Nat
Mi
Nat

Ode

Om
Part
Pira
Plak
Prop

Trains

BY HAL ROGERS

The Child's World

Published by The Child's World®
1980 Lookout Drive • Mankato, MN 56003-1705
800-599-READ • www.childsworld.com

Acknowledgments
The Child's World®: Mary Berendes, Publishing Director
The Design Lab: Design
Jody Jensen Shaffer; Editing
Pamela J. Mitsakos: Photo Research

Photos
AlbertPego/iStock.com: 15; auremar/Shutterstock.
com: 12; Binkski/Shutterstock.com: 4; FreezingRain/
iStock.com: 19; Kenneth Sponsler/iStock.com: cover,
1; remik44992/iStock.com: 11; sgtphoto/iStock.
com: 8; silkwayrain/iStock.com: 20; Soft Tones
Photography/iStock.com: 7; winhorse/iStock.com: 16

ISBN 9781623239725
LCCN 2013947258

Printed in the United States of America
Mankato, MN
November, 2013
PA02190

Contents

Trains have been used to move things for many years.

What are trains?

Trains are **vehicles** that move along a track. Train cars travel along metal rails. The cars are hooked together in a line.

How are trains used?

Passenger trains take people from place to place. These trains have seats and windows. Some passenger trains travel long distances. They often have a dining car where people can eat. They sometimes have sleeping cars, too.

This train carries people in London, England.

Freight cars come in many shapes and sizes.

Other trains carry goods, or **freight**. Freight trains carry heavy loads for long distances. Different types of freight cars carry different kinds of goods.

Some freight cars keep food cool. Some carry big metal boxes that hold lots of goods. Others have bins for carrying coal or other rock. Some have air holes for carrying animals.

Trains can move lots of coal cars at once.

This engineer drives a passenger train in Europe.

12

Who drives a train?

A train's driver is called an **engineer**. The engineer sits in the **cab**. The cab has **controls** for running the train.

How do trains move?

Some train cars have their own **engine**. The engine provides power so the car can move. Other train cars are pulled or pushed by a **locomotive**. Locomotives have big, powerful engines. They can pull lots of weight.

Locomotives are powerful enough to pull lots of cars at once.

This train runs on electricity. It gets its power from the wires above it.

Many train engines get their power from burning **diesel fuel**. Others get their power from **electricity**. Sometimes the electricity comes through overhead wires. Sometimes it comes through a rail on the track.

Most trains have metal wheels on the bottom. The wheels roll along metal rails. Some trains do not have wheels. Instead, magnets hold them above the rails.

This train in Germany uses magnets to move.

19

This type of train in China can reach speeds of 185 miles per hour (about 290 kph).

Are trains important?

Trains are used all over the world. They carry heavy goods over long distances. They take people from place to place quickly. Trains are very important!

GLOSSARY

cab (KAB) A machine's cab is the area where the driver sits.

controls (kun-TROHLZ) Controls are parts that people use to run a machine.

diesel fuel (DEE-sul FYOOL) Diesel fuel is a heavy oil that is burned to make power.

electricity (ee-lek-TRI-si-tee) Electricity is a kind of power or energy.

engine (EN-jun) An engine is a machine that makes something move.

engineer (en-jun-EER) On trains, an engineer is a person who runs the engine.

freight (FRAYT) Freight is a name for goods carried on a ship, plane, train, or truck.

locomotive (loh-kuh-MOH-tiv) A locomotive is a train car that can push or pull other cars.

passenger (PASS-un-jur) A passenger is a person who rides in something.

vehicles (VEE-uh-kulz) Vehicles are things for carrying people or goods.

BOOKS

Balkwill, Richard. *The Best Book of Trains*. New York: Kingfisher, 1999.

Harding, Mary, and Richard Courtney (illustrator). *All Aboard Trains*. New York: Platt & Munk, 1989.

National Railway Museum. *Big Book of Trains*. New York: DK Publishing, 1998.

Simon, Seymour. *Seymour Simon's Book of Trains*. New York: HarperCollins Publishers, 2004.

WEB SITES

Visit our Web site for lots of links about trains:
childsworld.com/links

Note to parents, teachers, and librarians: We routinely check our Web links to make sure they're safe, active sites—so encourage your readers to check them out!

INDEX

ABOUT THE AUTHOR

Hal Rogers has written over a dozen books on machines and trucks. A longtime resident of Colorado, Hal currently lives in Denver, along with his family, a fuzzy cat named Simon, and a lovable dog named Sebastian.